To

A gift wrapped in my
love and best wishes

From

A Mother's Joys

Loving Reflections

PUBLICATIONS INTERNATIONAL, LTD.

Original inspirations by Barbara Briggs Morrow.

Compiled inspirations by Cathy Tell.

Copyright © 1998 Publications International, Ltd. All
rights reserved. This publication may not be reproduced
or quoted in whole or in part by any means whatsoever
without written permission from:

Louis Weber, C.E.O.
Publications International, Ltd.
7373 North Cicero Avenue
Lincolnwood, Illinois 60646

Permission is never granted for commercial purposes.

Manufactured in China.

8 7 6 5 4 3 2 1

ISBN: 0-7853-2285-X

*W*hen God thought of mother, He must have laughed with satisfaction . . . so rich, so deep, so divine, so full of soul, power, and beauty, was the conception.

HENRY WARD BEECHER

A mother's arms
are made of tenderness
and children sleep
soundly in them.

VICTOR HUGO

*I*f a mother took time to compile a mothering resume, it would be one of the most impressive around. The first entry might read something like: "Human potential expert—responsible for all aspects of developing human beings from concept through final production."

Sometimes the best
and most difficult advice
a mother can give her
grown children is none.

You may have tangible
wealth untold;
Caskets of jewels and coffers of
gold.
Richer than I you can never
be—
I had a Mother who read to me.

STRICKLAND GILLIAN

I begin to love this little creature, and to anticipate his birth as a fresh twist to a knot, which I do not wish to untie.

MARY WOLLSTONECRAFT, IN A LETTER TO HER HUSBAND, WILLIAM GODWIN

My mother is a patient woman. For years, she taught knitting to adolescents. That says it all. She had seven children by age thirty, has fourteen grandchildren now, in her midfifties. When the noise and heat of young lives overwhelm her, she still cans tomatoes. When she was frustrated, she used to press the pedal of her sewing machine flat, sending the needle into a manic frenzy. She never lashed out at a child. That lesson is profound.

LOUISE ERDRICH

"How are you?"
From your mother, it's
never a casual question.
No matter how old you
are, she really wants to
know.

As a mother, I must faithfully, patiently, lovingly, and happily do my part—then quietly wait for God to do His.

RUTH BELL GRAHAM

Her chubby hands crept
round my neck
And whispered words I can't forget.
They cast a light upon my soul—
On secrets no one knew.
They startled me, I hear them yet:
"Someday I'll be like you!"

UNKNOWN

The hand that rocks the cradle is the hand that rules the world.

WILLIAM ROSS WALLACE

My mother wanted me to be her wings, to fly as she never quite had the courage to do. I love her for that. I love the fact that she wanted to give birth to her own wings.

ERICA JONG

God could not be
everywhere and therefore
he made mothers.

JEWISH PROVERB

*M*y Dear Mary,

How lonely the house seems—I never knew before how well you helped to fill it. I am anxious to hear of your first impressions of the city and how you like your new home. Ever since you went away, I have been wondering if it was as hard for you to go out into the world as it was for me to have you go. Don't write short, hurried letters, simply stating facts in their tersest form, but tell me all your thoughts and dreams and plans, your

❧

worries and trials, and we will talk them
over as two comrades.... If there is
anything in my life that can be of value
to you, I want you to have it; if I can save
you a stumble or a single false step, I
want to do it, but the only way I can do it
is to know your heart.

Your loving mother.

FLORENCE WENDEROTH SAUNDERS,
LETTERS TO A BUSINESS GIRL, 1908

Who ran to help
me when I fell,
And would some pretty
story tell,
Or kiss the place to make
it well?
My mother.

ANN TAYLOR

A daughter carries her mother's wisdom like a pocket-sized, ever-handy sewing kit. She's grateful to be able to pull it out for emergency repairs as well as for leisurely embroidery.

The tie which links mother and child is of such pure and immaculate strength as to be never violated. Holy, simple, and beautiful in its construction, it is the emblem of all we can imagine of fidelity and truth.

WASHINGTON IRVING

*M*y mother was the most beautiful woman I ever saw. All I am I owe to my mother. I attribute all my success in life to the moral, intellectual, and physical education I received from her.

GEORGE WASHINGTON

All that I am or
hope to be, I owe to my
angel mother.

ABRAHAM LINCOLN

This is a moment I deeply wish my parents could have lived to share. In the first place my father would have enjoyed what you have so generously said of me—and my mother would have believed it.

LYNDON B. JOHNSON,
COMMENCEMENT ADDRESS AT
BAYLOR UNIVERSITY, 1956

*D*ear Mother: I'm all
right. Stop worrying
about me.

EGYPTIAN PAPYRUS LETTER, CIRCA
2000 B.C.

One form of heroism—the most common, and yet the least remembered of all—namely, the heroism of the average mother. Ah! When I think of that broad fact, I gather hope again for poor humanity; and this dark world looks bright...because, whatever else it is not full of, it is at least full of mothers.

CHARLES KINGSLEY

The young mother hates to admit that she actually is sorry when her baby starts sleeping through the night. She will miss those still, focused minutes in the morning's wee hours when she and her little one cuddled in the big armchair, delighted to have the world and each other all to themselves for just a while.

There are only two things a child will share willingly—communicable diseases and his mother's age.

ATTRIBUTED TO DR. BENJAMIN SPOCK

A mother
understands what a child
does not say.

JEWISH PROVERB

A mother always has to think twice, once for herself and once for her child.

SOPHIA LOREN

My mother had a great deal of trouble with me, but I think she enjoyed it.

MARK TWAIN

And so because you love me,
and because
I love you, Mother, I have woven a wreath
Of rhymes wherewith to crown your
honoured name;
In you not fourscore years can dim the
flame
Of love, whose blessed glow transcends
the laws
Of time and change and mortal life and
death.

CHRISTINA ROSSETTI

My doctors told me I would never walk, but my mother told me I would, so I believed my mother.

WILMA RUDOLPH

As a mother yourself, you are startled to hear your own Mom's words coming out of your mouth, words you swore you would never say. What's really scary is "because I said so" now makes perfect sense.

*A*s a child, you couldn't help but be skeptical when, on her birthday, Mom said that the gift she wanted most was to celebrate with her family. You kept prodding to discover some hidden wish.

A flannel nightgown? A bottle of perfume? Then, years later, as a mother yourself, you discover she wasn't hiding a thing. Now, you both treasure the best gift of all.

*I*t was Mother who fought. Fought! To keep me up to par! To make me study and improve. Fought! To keep my name in the large type she believed I merited. Fought for heat in trains to protect my health. Fought to make ends meet, when each week she had finished sending money to the many dependents that automatically arrived on the high heels of success. Invincible! best describes her.

ELSIE JANIS

Some are kissing mothers and some are scolding mothers, but it is love just the same, and most mothers kiss and scold together.

PEARL BUCK

Women know
The way to rear up children (to be just),
They know a simple, merry, tender knack
Of tying sashes, fitting baby-shoes,
And stringing pretty words that make no
sense,
And kissing full sense into empty words.

ELIZABETH BARRETT BROWNING

A mother is not to
be compared with
another person—she is
incomparable.

AFRICAN PROVERB

The cologne, a gift from her daughter, brings to mind sun-dappled gardens and cool, soothing breezes. "It made me think of you," the daughter explains. The mother is speechless with gratitude for both gifts—the cologne and her daughter's thought.

*M*y mother raised
me, and then freed me.

MAYA ANGELOU

A MOTHER'S JOYS